San Miguel's Mexican Interiors

Sandy Baum

Schiffer Publishing Ltd

4880 Lower Valley Road Atlgen, Pennsylvania 19310

Other Schiffer Books on Related Subjects:
Mexican Popular Art: Clothing & Dolls, Wendy Scalzo
Mexican Folk Art: From Oaxacan Artist Families, Arden Rothstein &
    Anya Rothstein
Traditional Mexican Style Exteriors, Donna McMenamin
Mexican Style Sustainable, Tina Skinner

Copyright © 2008 by Sandy Baum
Library of Congress Control Number: 2007938149

Designed by John P. Cheek
Cover design by Bruce Waters

Type set in Lydian BT/Dutch809 BT

ISBN: 978-0-7643-2947-0
Printed in China

Published by Schiffer Publishing Ltd.
4880 Lower Valley Road
Atglen, PA 19310
Phone: (610) 593-1777; Fax: (610) 593-2002
E-mail: Info@schifferbooks.com

For the largest selection of fine reference books on this and related subjects, please visit our web site at **www.schifferbooks.com**
We are always looking for people to write books on new and related subjects. If you have an idea for a book please contact us at the above address.

This book may be purchased from the publisher.
Include $3.95 for shipping.
Please try your bookstore first.
You may write for a free catalog.

In Europe, Schiffer books are distributed by
Bushwood Books
6 Marksbury Ave.
Kew Gardens
Surrey TW9 4JF England
Phone: 44 (0) 20 8392-8585; Fax: 44 (0) 20 8392-9876
E-mail: info@bushwoodbooks.co.uk
Website: www.bushwoodbooks.co.uk
Free postage in the U.K., Europe; air mail at cost.

Contents

Acknowledgments ✋ *Reconocimiento*

San Miguel de Allende has been my home for the last three years. I was attracted to its laid-back ambience, the cosmopolitan (big city small town) atmosphere, the architecture, and the quiet magic that seems to permeate the air we breathe. There is a creative community made up of artists of every persuasion including writers, sculptors, painters and photographers just to name a few. This town thrives on the creativity found here.

In putting together San Miguel's Mexican Interiors, my intent was to present a variety of homes, ranging from the Spanish-Colonial era with what some homeowners have done within their 350 year old homes, to today, in homes that have been built or remodeled in the last ten years.

This book would not have been possible without the generosity of the San Miguel homeowners who open their homes every Sunday for the House and Garden tours sponsored by San Miguel's Biblioteca Publica. Limited space here, however, does not permit the listing of all those generous individuals.

A special thanks to my two editors at Schiffer Publishing, Ltd., Nancy Schiffer and Tina Skinner, for having the patience and foresight to help me see this book to completion.

I hope you, the reader, enjoy the journey into these colorful homes through my camera's eye, a view that is not available to the average San Miguel visitor.

Introduction ❧ *Introduccíon*

San Miguel, one of the oldest towns in Mexico, began about the time silver was discovered in Mexico in 1542. San Miguel became famous not for silver mining, but as a commercial stop-over for the silver laden wagons coming from other mining towns to the north and west, on their way to Queretaro and continuing on to Mexico City. During the period of silver mining, San Miguel grew into a city of wealth and extravagance. The population swelled and as a result the town was renamed San Miguel el Grande. This was the period when many of the magnificent homes in "El Centro" were built. After years of exploitation, the silver mines petered out and San Miguel went into a slow decline with the population dwindling to around 5,000 persons. It wasn't until after the war for independence from Spain was over, that the town's name was changed to honor its fallen hero, Ignacio Allende.

The streets of San Miguel de Allende are a treasure trove of Colonial style architecture, betraying a strong Spanish influence with their grand archways and dramatic staircases. The traditional architecture of San Miguel revolves around a central courtyard just inside the entry *zaguan*, adjacent to the street. Outside walls have few if any openings and access through the entry into the courtyard from the street is secured by massive wood doors or iron gates. In the early days, horse-drawn wagons with their precious silver cargo entered the courtyards, remaining overnight or longer, protected from any band of outlaws who may have had thoughts regarding this cargo. Today, automobiles have replaced the wagons in the courtyards. In homes with access to the roof, a finished covered terrace is a valuable architectural element providing additional place for outdoor entertaining, generally with wonderful views of the city.

San Miguel sits at a 6,000 foot elevation where the air is clear and the sunlight bright with sharp shadows. The days are sunny and warm; the skies are a cobalt blue, (a brighter blue, many think, than in Santa Fe, New Mexico). You would expect the climate at 6,000 feet to be cold all the time, but not here in the hill country where San Miguel is situated. The average year-round temperature is 75 degrees. Daytime temperatures in summer can reach into the low 90's, but the nights cool down significantly. On winter days, the temperature climbs into the high 70's while nights sometimes drop down into the mid 30's. Without central heating, some of the winter months can get quite chilly before the sun warms the day. The traditional San Miguel house has separate fireplaces in many of the rooms which help to alleviate the cold. For some, winter is also a good time to have an electric blanket available for those excessively cold nights. The rainy season usually arrives in late June, lasting into August. The rain is generally brief with sunshine by the end of the day. A profusion of wild flowers blankets the surrounding countryside in the aftermath of the rainy season.

In the early days, trees were not plentiful and construction lumber was not readily available in the San Miguel area. Until recently, most homes in San Miguel had been constructed using methods dating back to the seventeenth century; only the materials have changed through the years. In those early days, adobe was the material of choice. It was plentiful, easy to make and the erection process was straight forward. Mix in a little straw with mud and water, pour into a form, let dry in the sun for several days and presto, you have a building block. The adobe was lighter than stones found in the area and because of their shape, were easier to utilize. Also, adobe blocks could be made on site while the rocks had to be quarried and hauled to the building. Adobe, a universal and ancient material, was simple, efficient, economical and expressive with excellent color and texture.

Another favorite material, discovered to be plentiful in the local area, was *cantera*, a volcanic stone. In early Mexican history there was much volcanic activity. *Cantera* was found to have a structural capacity provided by no other material available at that time. Wood was not plentiful and would have had to be carted a great distance, which for those early times in Mexico, was not practical or cost effective. Workmen found that *cantera* had the ability to support great weights, which enabled the construction of second floors through the use of arches, columns, door and window frames made of this stone. Today, *cantera* is used mostly for embellishments rather than structural. Concrete and re-bar are now used for the structural integrity of many-storied residential buildings with various forms of masonry units such as brick, concrete blocks, adobe and others as fill-ins between the structural concrete elements.

After the adobe walls were completed, a plaster-like material was used to cover the adobe to protect the walls from the elements. This material had to be replaced frequently as it would flake off, exposing the adobe to the elements which would cause the individual adobe bricks to disintegrate. It didn't take long for the walls to crumble if the protective coat was allowed to go unattended.

The traditional house design incorporated a courtyard surrounded by the house structure. Zero lot lines did not allow walls with windows looking out on adjacent properties. Therefore, all the natural light for the living quarters came from the open courtyard. Later, skylights were introduced in the form of cupolas, rounded dome structures with vertical glass built into the sides, which also brought light from the roof areas allowing the light to reach dark corners in the rooms below. Today, glass blocks, or *translucents* are set into the roof structure, lighting up the areas below as well.

In the hands of today's young architects, the traditional home designs have taken on a whole new direction. Using the same materials as their forefathers, they are creating architectural art, weaving the materials into sensual elegant structures.

Chapter 1
Doors ᦥ *Puertas*

Doors create the first impression of "what's to come" as one enters a San Miguel residence in the Spanish-Colonial era built homes. The entry area, called a *zaguan*, which is immediately inside the main entrance door, connects the front of the house to the central courtyard. Today's newly designed homes, inside as well as outside the central core, have taken on a more contemporary motif, almost eliminating the entry, with the visitor entering through the front door into the courtyard which is surrounded by the living quarters of the residence.

Here in San Miguel, doors come in a variety of woods from pine (easy to carve) to alder and mesquite (very heavy).

This vehicle door also houses the entry into this home. The door knocker along with the mail slot denotes this as the main entrance.

Far left:
An exquisitely carved double door with carved transom, brick arch and inlaid *talavera* tile is sandwiched between a pair of *cantera* columns.

Left:
A double entrance door has a creative design cut into the brick surround. The individual triangular panels held in place with equally placed screws forming a unique design pattern using left-over materials.

This combination green door with lavender frame surrounded by a bright yellow wall and brightly colorful bougainvillea flowers is one of the many wondrous scenes found while walking in San Miguel.

This pair of four-panel doors framed by a *cantera* surround and an iron transom backed by a clerestory glass pane.

A six-panel double leaf door surrounded by a pink *cantera* stone frame set in a pink wall.

10

This main entrance leads into a foyer with a magnificent collection of folk art. The metal door and glass is accentuated by the stone and glass surround.

This multi-paneled double door with black iron straps to reinforce the door, continues as a design element, surrounded by pink *cantera* set in a yellow wall.

11

This main entrance consists of a pair of metal doors surrounded by stone on the exterior wall.

This double entry with its elegantly designed ironwork with the *talavera* house sign identifies the owners within.

This double glass-paneled entry door opens immediately into the courtyard beyond. The two coach lights on either side with the two potted plants add color to the entrance.

This multi-faceted carved and geometric door is surrounded by *cantera* stone imbedded in an exterior brick wall.

This garage door mimics the design of the wood entrance doors and the *cantera* arches.

A single geometric designed entry door provides access to the garden beyond sandwiched between two *cantera* columns and door frame.

This double-arched entry surrounds a six-panel door with iron and glass transom. Surrounding the opening is a hand-painted frieze.

This double entry door handsomely carved with a pink *cantera* surround, door knocker and mail slot, indicate this is the main entrance.

Green foliage in front of this pink wall and *cantera* framed windows on either side balance this main entry.

This uniquely carved double door set in a green wall framed by a pair of *cantera* columns is further enhanced by the potted plants and other foliage.

Another garage door with the main entrance inset in the larger door with its mail slot, door knocker and peep hole covered with a wire mesh.

This pair of ten foot high carriage doors with the wood beam header and transom above may be part of the original 300 year old structure with the main entry door in the left leaf.

This six-panel door with its carved figure eights surrounded by a lavender surround, framed by two carriage lights, is actually a door to nowhere mounted on an exterior wall.

With the door behind, this *cantera* surround was a later add-on.

15

This inviting entrance flanked by two coach lights still retains the hitching ring from a former mode of transportation.

This deeply recessed eight-paneled door is surrounded by a massive stone wall enhanced by the green foliage.

This four-paneled striated entrance door is flanked by two coach lights on a pink wall with pre-cast concrete mimicking *cantera*.

This hand-carved *cantera* surrounding the entrance leads into an outdoor foyer with lush foliage.

It's not unusual to find old doors used in new construction. Behind this wall, originally a ruin, is now contains a clever use of space.

Chapter 2
Living Rooms ⌘ *Salas*

Living rooms evoke a sense of welcome and are generally an expression of the personality of the owners. Living rooms are a place where family and friends feel instantly at home. The best designed or furnished spaces communicate warmth. Living rooms come in all sizes and shapes. Nowhere are there two alike. Maybe the colors are similar, but that's where any similarity ends. Some home owners have brought their furniture with them, and along with items bought in their travels throughout Mexico and the world, have created a home style that is a cross between traditional Mexican architectural interiors and familiar comfortable surroundings.

A profusion of bright Mexican colors are mixed and matched in this informal *sala*. Above the tiled front of the corner fireplace, Virgin of Guadalupe inspires the color scheme.

The seating is plush upholstered *equipale* (pigskin). An old door is used as a table-top. The lamp table is also old with some of the original paint visible.

Floor to ceiling windows and arches open these rooms and add drama. Wood strips add to the pattern of the floor tiles.

Here light neutral colors have been used with blue as an accent color. The lighted *nichos* are great for special collectibles. Floors are *saltillo* tile.

Comfortable seating is arranged to enjoy a wall of the owner's paintings which continue into the dining area. Textured pillows complement the conversation area rug.

A skylight highlights the lavender wall and objects of art. The stone coffee table from China is bordered with wood. The chair at the end of the dining table is from Ethiopia. An ornate tin mirror adds another perspective to the room. The floors are white wood.

A simple, basically neutral sala with a colorful table runner that complements the framed art.

This intimate seating area has elements of multiple textures from the wall block *sillar*, rug used as wall hanging, various textured pillows, wood tables, metal and glass table, and area rug. Tin and black pottery adds accents.

The cozy conversational seating is backed with a drop leaf table and locally made iron floor lamp.

Equipale table and chairs along with upholstered equipale sofa are used in this informal *sala*. Painted lacquer and folk art accessories are on the wooden coffee table and painted cupboard.

A display of local pewter and other collectibles is carefully displayed in this *sala*. A traditional tin chandelier and the beamed ceiling is reflected in the plastered shell *concha* mirror.

Blue and yellow, wood and wicker are combined within the painted, patterned lower wall which frames the room.

This home is part of an old factory which has been renovated and has kept the original floors and pipes framing the dining area window. The large polo player painting fits the two story room.

Tan, orange, and bright yellow are repeated in this small seating area. A small pillow by the Cuna Indians of Panama is a centered accent.

The *cantera* fireplace is surrounded by intimate seating to watch the fire or TV. The round tabletop adds an artistic flair.

An oxen yoke goes well with the wooden beam mantel on the adobe brick in this large informal *sala*. Blue upholstered *equipale* chairs accent the neutral colored room.

This *sala* has soft hues, traditional furnishings, a plastered shell over the shelves besides the fireplace, and a classic tin chandelier. *Pulque* balls accent accessories on the mantel in this formal setting.

Multiple windows add spaciousness to this large contemporary seating area.

A tin lamp fills the arch in the *sillar* wall. The black pottery is from Oaxaca. Another sitting area is seen outside.

Looking down on an inviting *sala* seating area with Asian accents. The rug is particularly interesting in this setting.

Looking through the living room towards the study *estudio*, we see that the colors are repeated from one room to the next. A half bath is seen through the opened door. All rooms open to garden areas.

Blue saints stand by the owner's painting on an ancient cupboard in the dining area. The rarely needed fireplace *chimenea* is between the open living and dining area.

Every seat in this *sala*, faces the outdoors. Extra lavender pillows add color to the deep, comfortable couch and chairs.

Extra couch pillows pick up rug and drapery colors. An ancient cupboard has a special place.

This outdoor seating of *equipale* turquoise and lavender pigskin leather is even more colorful against the bright orange wall. A large painted iguana adds a whimsical touch.

A stone wall is often left unfinished for a special effect. Here the cement base, upholstered, built in seating, wooden table, woven mat, and accessories suggest an Asian look.

29

Warm earth tones on walls, the rug, and tile floor as well as on the upholstered *equipale* furniture, pictures, and clay figures on the warm wood table are very inviting.

A combination dining area and living room shows off the marble table top on wrought iron legs. The walls are painted faux green and large candle holders are on either side of the *cantera* fireplace.

Looking towards the living room from the study *studio*, the lavender accent colors in the yellow *sala* are the main color for this room. The white twisted columns help define the areas. High gloss tile floors are softened by the rugs used in each room.

The colors of the painting on the terracotta colored wall are repeated in the accent pillows.

The fireplace wall was especially built for this Buddha and other objects of art from the owners' travels.

Color and folk art combine in interesting ways. The table lamp is "herringbone" design tile. The angel, dance mask and costume are highlighted by the track lightning. A woven jaguar is used as an end table.

A skylight was added between beams of the old beamed ceiling and shutters were replaced when the room was re-painted. Older dark tile floors were left in this formal *sala*.

31

Typical glass paned doors open to an outside sitting area. The soft green crushed velvet couches, *cantera* fireplace, and antiques make this a classic *sala*.

Another view of a formal living room *sala* with well-lit artwork.

Looking down on an inviting reading area, we are drawn to the warm colors of the rug, pillows, painting, and wall.

Plaids and floral designs of greens and pinks are combined to make a colorful statement.

This is a formal *sala* with large matching pots and lamps. The seating is around the fireplace. Mexican pewter is on the table behind the sofa.

Chapter 3
Kitchens ❧ Cocínas

Kitchens are busy places, more so if the kitchen is small. Most Mexican kitchens are anything but small. They are quite open, with much activity gravitating in and around them. For many, the kitchen is frequently the most used room in the home. All too often, the kitchen serves as a casual entertaining area where the sights, sounds and smells provide a relaxed atmosphere for family and guests alike. To aid in keeping kitchens clean, tile is used throughout; for counter tops and backsplashes, *talavera* tile, and for floors, *saltillo* tile. As a result, spills of most any kind are easy to clean up. Lately, other hard materials have been introduced for keeping surfaces clean such as marble, granite and steel-troweled concrete.

Blue and white tile emphasized by blue grout sits on top of matching blue base and wall cabinets above. A galley kitchen lacking wall space, dictates the need to hang pots and pans from the ceiling.

A skylight provides light for this inside galley style kitchen. A center island with polished concrete top provides additional work space as well as storage below.

This galley style kitchen is tiled from counter to ceiling around the dark stained beams.

An open style kitchen is decorated with blue and white patterned and plain *talavera* tiles with white cabinets and cupboards and warm wood counter tops. Small blue and white tiles accent the *saltillo* floor tiles.

This colorful kitchen is an eye catcher painted blue, bright pink, green, and turquoise. *Saltillo* tile has been used on the counter tops.

Traditional *talavera* patterned tiles and white cupboards are often combined with yellow for a crisp, clean look. An old wooden table with colorful painted chairs adds a functional accent.

Herringbone patterned tiles form the stove backdrop and are flanked by open cupboards for a contemporary look. Counter tops are stained concrete.

This kitchen is a colorful country style.

Every color of the glassware was used in painting this kitchen.

This close-up of a colorful kitchen accent shows the popular cross and heart pattern on the painted chairs.

A view of an oval kitchen from above shows contemporary black granite countertops and white walls and floors.

The tablecloth picks up the bright yellow walls and painted green fixture filled with blue and white *talavera* dishes and pottery serving pieces.

This kitchen has a clean, spacious workspace. The cupboard with a glass door adds interest as do the ceramic pieces. The ceiling is beamed and floors are brick.

The glassware is a functional, colorful kitchen decoration.

39

The *boveda* brick ceiling, punched tin hanging lamp, and completely tiled walls are classic Mexican style. The blue molding is made from concrete to look like painted wood. This is commonly done as wood is scarce and expensive.

A hood over the stove in a Mexican kitchen can have a fan or be merely decorative. The *nicho* is decorative and useful. The table provides a well lighted work or eating area.

This side of this open kitchen has additional counter space. The floor is a combination of hexagon shaped tiles and small square tiles.

Plain colored tiles are often used in angled stripes or "saw tooth" patterns as shown in this kitchen. To make these patterns, a *talavera* tile is cut at a 45-degree angle and usually used with a contrasting color. It is called *medio-panuelo* meaning half-hand-kerchief.

This step-saver kitchen has everything at hand. Decorative ceramic plates are occasionally used as serving pieces. Counter top and floor is *saltillo* tile.

The bands of yellow and red tiles interwoven with the green wall tiles add a highlight to this kitchen.

These bright blue base and wall cabinets create a great color combination with the green tiles. The red door pulls are a nice addition.

The yellow and red wall pattern is repeated on the face of the hood above the range.

The classic blue and white in an older style high ceiling kitchen with *nichos* under the counter for storage. The custom designed tiles were made in Puebla.

This kitchen is the brightest possible pink. The floral painting is eye catching as well.

Popular blue bird tiles are used as stove backsplash. There is a design change on the hood over the stove where plain blue and a smaller bird tile define the change of pattern from "diamond" to square.

43

Chapter 4
Dining Rooms ⁊ *Comedores*

The size of the dining table surrounded by any number of chairs is dependent on the size of the dining room and the family needs. Also, entertaining obligations may alter those same requirements.

Dining rooms traditionally adjacent to the kitchen are located in a central space facing the courtyard separated by glass doors, French or otherwise. For entertaining purposes or large gatherings, these doors when fully opened, include the dining room in the house's large open interior area around the courtyard.

An upholstered cement bench adds interest and additional seating. The drapes can close off the kitchen for company.

The tin topped dining table and old cupboard, extra rattan chairs, reds and orange make this more than just a dining area.

Dining inside here is like eating in the garden. Chairs, upholstered differently, sit well together. Decorations include a large *talavera* vase and an interesting mask collection.

Neutral furnishings are used with colorful place settings and center piece. A pine buffet is on the back wall and green ceramic pineapple is on the floor beside it.

This formal dining room features a tapestry on the back wall. The punched tin star light hangs from a plastered *boveda* ceiling between the dining room *comedor* and living room *sala*. Arches are framed with local *cantera*. Masks on rods and ceramic pineapple are seen on the way from one room to another. An open doorway leads to the kitchen.

46

The painted green faux walls, folding screen, beautiful *saltillo* floor tiles and traditional tin chandelier provide a Mexican feeling to this dining area.

In the upper left corner, the old step seat with window to the street is updated to be used as extra seating for this small dining area. The mirror and glass table top help make the room seem larger.

A rich, dark Spanish style table is set with comfortable dark leather chairs. An antique cupboard sits by traditional shuttered windows with the built in seat for watching the street.

Different bright colors come together and are complemented by the lamp and table settings. The carved wood wall hanging and tin chandelier add interesting detail.

This view from above shows *saltillo* tile floor, a sideboard with Mexican pewter accessories, an oval table, and second blue lamp.

A Mexican style dining table with high backed *equipale* chairs is used with an antique carved buffet.

A glass topped table in the dining area is separated from the studio by a wooden cupboard. A wood beamed ceiling and shell *concha* are seen over the shelves by the arched doorway to the kitchen.

This open dining room *comedor* has a long buffet for storage with a large metal framed mirror over it and round conversational dining for six. The floor tiles have been treated to look old. An interesting metal chandelier is suspended from the *boveda* ceiling.

This is a small
dining area
furnished with a
wooden table top
on twisted iron
legs and wooden
shelf wall mount-
ed on wrought
iron brackets.
The stone wall
has been painted.
The accessories
are popular tin
mirrors, ceramic
pineapples, and
candle holders.

Chapter 5
Bedrooms ❧ Recamaras

Bedrooms are for sleeping, entertaining or otherwise relaxing away from an active home environment. Beds with carved ornate headboards usually occupy the central focus in most bedrooms. Colorful Mexican designed bedspreads brighten the rooms. Sunlight enters thru glass blocks, *translucents*, built into the ceiling above, lighting deep recesses in the bedrooms, casting ever changing shadows on the walls.

Painted stripes look like wallpaper in this traditionally furnished and decorated master bedroom *recamara principal*.

The red wall and paint-
ing make this a dramatic
bedroom.

This bedroom has been painted
bright green and features the
painting over the bed. The small
chest at the foot of the bed is a
nice extra touch.

Angels hover for protection on faux painted and trimmed blue wall just over the elaborately carved headboard in this master bedroom *recamara principal*.

The dark carved headboard looks perfect on the golden orange faux painted walls in this bedroom.

A bark paper wall hanging is featured over this green and gold bedroom.

This is a neutral colored guest bedroom with Mexican accessories and classic tin mirror.

Here, yellow, red, and orange combine on the wall and the bed. There are carved pine nightstands and indigenous clothing hangs on the wall.

This bedroom features a red headboard and patterned pillows.

The colorful patterned pillows add comfort to the sitting area of a master bedroom *recamara principal*. The view outside is also inviting.

Bedrooms are also private retreats and often have intimate sitting areas. A large "tree of life" adds interest on the *cantera* fireplace mantel.

A light and airy look with decorative netting and tin tree over the headboards. The pink and green colors are picked up in the embroidered piece from Puebla on the top of the bed.

The ornate wrought iron four poster bed with crosses atop the posts surrounds the bed while the different colored pastel sheers add a feeling of intimacy. Angel based lamps are shown on the night stands, an incense burner hangs from the top railing, and a tin framed mirror is over the headboard.

Warm greens, dark wood, and yellow, with a bit of red combine in a comfortable bedroom.

This is a simpler wrought iron bed again with crosses on the four posts and a sheer canopy. Angel bedside lamps have punched tin shades for a star effect. A painting of church domes hangs nearby and an incense burner on a bedpost completes the scene.

The dark purple wall high-lights this contemporary bedroom.

Dark wood and walls give this room an old Spanish look.

This iron four poster bed has a soft drape behind the headboard which defines the bed from the stone wall behind it. The comfortable desk chair is called "poor man's *equipale*" because it uses wood instead of pigskin.

Hand carved bed posts go beautifully with the sewn together indigenous clothing *wipils* from Guatemala as a bedspread.

The carved wooden four poster bed and surrounding décor suggest a sophisticated country look.

The *boveda* ceiling and warm colors of the room are very Mexican. A TV area is seen through the archway and part of a sitting area is seen across from the bed with hand carved post and hand sewn indigenous fabric *wipils* from Guatemala as a bedspread.

60

An antique opium headboard from China and oriental ceramic lamp from the homeowner's travels are used in this bedroom.

A special piece of fabric has been framed behind glass and used as a headboard in this soft green and pink bedroom.

A rainbow of color welcomes guests on their stay in San Miguel de Allende. Folk art and hand woven fabrics fill the room and the hand carved headboards complete the picture.

A carved, painted headboard shows angels watching over day and night. The bedside cupboards repeat the day and night theme. A rainbow is also suggested.

This view shows a painting of arches over the bed and several colorful textured pillows.

The concrete shelf headboard is useful and decorative in this contemporary bedroom.

Sheer drapes partly cover the large mirror headboard. The *equipale* chairs and table at the bottom of the bed face a fireplace across the room. A fabric hanging is on the plain wall.

This is a classic bedroom with a four poster bed.

An ornate wrought iron headboard shows nicely on the blue faux wall. Bedside lamps are *talavera* ceramic.

A local tin framed mirror is hung over the oriental chest between the beds in this bedroom. An old yoke and carved wooden angels are other Mexican touches. The built-in vanity with *talavera* tiles is convenient for guests.

A chest with a quilt on it sits across the room and inspired the home owner to paint it and use it as a headboard in this guest room.

The green throw on the bed goes nicely with the color in this bedroom and the red lamp shades are an interesting accent.

The Mexican painted nightstands are a nice touch in this traditional bedroom.

A special floral fabric wall hanging adds color to the neutral bedroom. A garden waits just outside the door.

A comfortable bedroom awaits the guests.

The carved headboard and nightstands and indigenous fabric bed cover are very Mexican and often used in bedrooms with blue faux walls.

Chapter 6
Bathrooms ⤐ Baños

Bathrooms come in a variety of shapes and sizes and colors, especially when *talavera* tiles are used. With an eye to color and design, bathrooms receive a great deal of thought, especially if a tub is to be included for those luxuriant times, soaking in bubbles, while wiling away the time without a care in the world. With the use of *talavera* tile, anything goes. Bathrooms can run the gamut starting with a whimsical look or ending with a rich artistry. The end results are unlimited.

Talavera tiles in this bathroom *baño* are arranged in a diamond design on the wall and arranged differently behind the sink and on the front end of the counter.

Part of a bathroom *baño* showing floor to ceiling use of tile.

Here *talavera* tiles frame a mirror as well as cover the counter top.

Lots of light helps show off the tiled walls and counter top.

Punched tin light fixtures illuminate this bathroom *baño* with marble walls and scalloped marble counter top.

A Mexican star light hangs over the onyx bowl and a tin chandelier is centered in an archway of this master bath.

This concrete counter is covered in *talavera* tile with blue and white patterned tile covering the backsplash and surrounding the mirror with a louvered front on the base cabinet below..

The walls of this shower are steel-trowel concrete. The concrete was then stained and polished. The floor of the shower is brick laid in concrete forming an unusual pattern matching the curved shower walls. An unusual showerhead has been added.

A contemporary looking bathroom uses marble instead of tile.

A popular floral pattern of *talavera* tile alternating with plain white is used throughout this bathroom.

Classic blue patterned and white *talavera* tile with plastered shell *concha* over mirror. The patterned sink is also *talavera* ceramic while a tin wall lamp lights the area.

The onyx basin was set into the concrete counter top on a pine cupboard base with paver accent added to the top.

The popular lily *cadencia* patterned blue *talavera* tiled sink is surrounded by white tiles. Plain blue tile edges the counter top and arches, while a different pattern finishes the bathroom.

A black granite counter top with two white oval bowls stand out in this grey painted bathroom.

Plain colored tiles and a tin framed mirror were chosen for this bathroom.

This all-concrete base cabinet supports a copper bowl inset into the concrete top, while shelves below store some bathroom necessities. White rocks embellish the front edges and the backsplash.

A contemporary black granite counter top has been used in this master bathroom with a rounded mirror.

The onyx bowls and wall fixtures make this a contemporary style bathroom.

A classic *talavera* pattern in the sink and tiles is again used with plain white. The mirror is framed with a tile border and ceramic water jug is handy in the corner.

A diamond pattern of tile has been used on the front edge of the counter. The unusual sink is set in the tile countertop.

A patterned border is used here with plain tiles.

Pink and blue have been repeated in paint and tile for a dramatic look.

This sophisticated bathroom uses neutral tiles and wood throughout. Using tiles straight below the sculptured border and changing to a diamond design above the border adds interest. The floor is also laid in the diamond design with a straight border.

Diamond designed tiles with straight ones as a border are finished with a white edging that complements the grout. The granite counter top picks up the tile color. Mexican bath tubs are often tile over concrete as is this one.

A plastered shell *concha* defines this bathroom. Patterned *talavera* tile is used on the counter top front edge and as a backsplash. A few of the patterned tiles have been added to the white tile countertop. A plain blue tile edges the sink and counter top. Brass fixtures and gold framed mirror finish this attractive area.

Yet another example of blue and white tiles and *talavera* sinks. A *talavera* ceramic water jug is in the corner.

A pine carved and painted cabinet holds the colored sink. The tiled wall behind it is a very Mexican look.

This master bathroom has pine cupboards, polished cement and brick counter top, onyx sinks, and tin framed mirrors. A water jug sits on a wooden stand.

An arched opening
is the entrance to a
colorful tiled shower.

The pattern of *talavera* tile used
on the back splash is repeated in
the border above the lights.

This shower sports a *talavera* area rug look-a-like.

An enlargement of the wall tile pattern shown on the next page.

This tub area is festooned with *talavera* tile.

The blue and white *talavera* tiles are mesmerizing. You might find yourself lulled toward sleeping it off in this Jacuzzi-type tub.

Chapter 7
Fireplaces ⚜ Chimeneas

Without central heating systems, many rooms in the San Miguel homes have fireplaces to offset the cold evenings during the winter months. Originally, the fireplaces were wood burning only. Today, many homes have been retrofitted with propane gas lines providing an alternate means to heating the home, as well as for cooking and creating hot water for bathing.

Today, you can still see firewood-laden donkeys walking the streets in search of customers who use wood in their kitchen stoves or fireplaces.

The city administration, in a program to keep any further trees from being cut down in the countryside, provides wood (from approved cut trees) to any interested parties for use in stoves or fireplaces.

This raised fireplace *chimenea* is made of concrete and brightly painted to stand out from the warm wood book cases and accent the room. The mantel provides a great place for the *mariachi* to perform.

The front of this raised fireplace has been tiled with "Mexican white" tiles and several floral *talavera* tiles possibly left over from another project.

An interesting corner fireplace covering two living areas. The shelf around the raised fireplace provides distance from the fire and a place for decorations. The brick pattern forms the hearth and is carried into the shelf.

A lion's head seems to leap out from the flames in this painted concrete corner fireplace. Two more lions are sentinels on the sides. The mantel is a mosaic of broken tile pieces

A plain cement fireplace with brick hearth and edging blends into this living room *sala* conversation area. The wall-mounted angels and carved cupboards add Mexican touches.

A wall-mounted cement fireplace with long shaped flue and decoration at the bottom of the *cantera* hearth.

Talavera tile decorates this raised corner fireplace.

The columns for this fireplace are painted cement. Instead of blending in, it stands out and is probably the conversation piece of the room.

The wooden beam is the perfect mantle for this adobe fireplace with raised extended hearth so someone can sit by the fire.

A hand painted design trims this corner fireplace.

While most fireplaces are propane, this is wood burning and so this larger corner fireplace has a screen. Crosses decorate the flue.

Fireplaces using carved *cantera* are classic and beautiful. The shell motif is common. This fireplace is off-season, but the wood is ready.

Cantera can also be plain instead of carved and the columns add a classic look.

This cement-formed fireplace is decorated with a special fabric hanging and lighted from above.

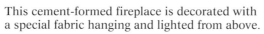

Angels fly over the painted concrete mantel for this raised wall inserted fireplace with sculpture on the sides.

A traditional carved *cantera* fireplace where an ornate candle holder has been placed for the off season. A pair of candle sticks rest on *cantera* bases on either side of the fireplace.

This is a large contemporary style wood-burning fireplace completely formed from concrete.

A large carved *cantera* fireplace high-lights this *sala*.

The popular blue bird patterned *talavera* tile has been used on the walls and lower part of this raised fireplace. The birds were painted on the front of the corner fireplace as well.

The *cantera* arched fireplace stands out from the purple wall.

Art objects have been added on and beside the colorful painted fireplace in this bedroom.

Here is a plain *cantera* mantel and fireplace for a traditional look.

This is an example of a gas fireplace of carved *cantera* which shows off nicely on the blue wall.

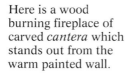

Here is a wood burning fireplace of carved *cantera* which stands out from the warm painted wall.

An interesting decorative piece fills the *nicho* above the fireplace in a contemporary setting.

This contemporary fireplace is built of *cantera* blocks. The skylight highlights this structure.

The treasured Buddha had a fireplace built just for him. The lighted *nicho* adds dimension and the fireplace front copies the plan.

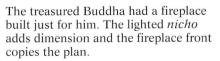

This screened corner fireplace has been stenciled up
the sides of the flue.

This *sala* has a carved and painted fireplace with columns on the side and angels
in the upper corners.

92

This wood burning small corner fireplace is plain yet sophisticated.

This corner wood-burning fireplace generates a great deal of warmth in the cold winter evenings.

This lavender and green fireplace adds a touch of whimsy to the living room. The green shelves on either side store some of the owners' folk art and book collection.

Chapter 8
Furniture ∾ Muebles

Many of the furniture pieces shown on the pages of this book have been hand-made by local carpenters, some working with modern tools and machinery. Many of the carved cabinet and door fronts were done with mallets and hand chisels. Artists use the utmost care to create a "one-of-a-kind" piece of furniture, while the resulting piece shows a love for their traditions and methods handed down over centuries.

A painted drop-leaf desk with drawers and cupboard is in the spotlight in this room. The painted scenes on the front show the artist's skill.

An *equipale* sofa has been paired with an interesting *equipale* table with twig top laid in a diamond pattern.

A small sturdy wooden bench with interesting details sits in the garden patio.

A hand carved outside chair has a cushion added for comfort.

A wood strip in a diamond pattern has been added to this simple wooden chest on legs. The top of the chest is decorated with religious folk art.

This tub-style chair has been carved out of wood.

Two *equipale* chairs with twig backs flank the handsomely carved bench. An old door with hinges is the table top.

A sturdy handmade wooden bench for outdoor seating with a bowed front piece adding interest.

These *equipale* chairs have unusual backs. A colorful straw mat acts as a table cloth on the *equipale* table.

High backed *equipale* chairs have cushions for added comfort. The pigskin is stretched on the table top and must be finished to be waterproof.

This ornately carved cupboard resembles a Spanish antique.

The unstained pine cupboard is carved and in two pieces.

The round outdoor table has woven chairs with seat cushions that match the brightly colored table cloth.

Wrought iron outdoor furniture is popular. The bright yellow cushions and striped pillows add a nice touch.

Some of the old green paint remains on this useful cupboard.

This carved cupboard has classic handles and is useful storage on the covered terrace *loggia*.

The mirror
frame is cactus.

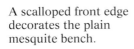 A scalloped front edge
decorates the plain
mesquite bench.

This small painted antique cupboard is useful in a
small space.

Right:
This antique armoire is even more beautiful with all it's hardware. It could be useful in any room of the house.

Far right:
Even the sides of this armoire are carved with the traditional shell motif.

The plush upholstered *equipale* chaise and oversized upholstered chair share the small round *equipale* table in this loggia.

Chapter 9
Lighting ✑ *Iluminacion*

Locally made lighting of all sizes and shapes awaits the homeowner. Hand made up-lighting, down-lighting, wall and stairway sconces, and chandeliers are available. You will find floor lamps, table lamps, hanging fixtures, all for the asking. If you have a design in mind but don't see what you want, produce a sketch or photograph, and return in a week or ten days for the completed piece.

This punched-tin hanging lantern is a favorite, casting multiple rays of light on the walls and floor.

A typical street lamp sans the glass sits forlornly waiting for the switch to be thrown.

The punched-tin star is a favorite, whether a single or in clusters.

A wall hanging light with wire mesh protects the light bulbs from wayward rocks.

105

This brass sconce lights up the stairwell casting beams down the walls.

This eighteen-light metal chandelier hangs from a painted barrel-vaulted ceiling centered over the living room.

An iron thirty-four light chandelier hangs over the dining table.

An outdoor wall hanging fixture.

A shaded twelve-light brass chandelier hangs in the center of the kitchen.

A massive punched-metal fixture hangs from the *boveda* ceiling.

A classic metal chandelier hangs from the *boveda* ceiling over the dining table.

Far left:
Brass with glass wall sconce is on outside patio.

Left:
Punched tin and glass lamp fixture hangs in dining room.

Standard outdoor wall fixture.

Punched-metal light shade hangs in kitchen over island work surface.

Glass and metal chandelier hangs in dining room.

This light illuminating the house address is one of two straddling the front entry.

A punched-metal sconce lights up the fountain at the end of the patio.

Metal and glass hanging lantern.

Custom made
metal coach light.

Metal wall hanger.

Exterior coach light illuminates walking area outside.

Moroccan-theme hanging fixture, one of many providing light in the courtyard.

Moroccan inspired floor lamp.

This multi-lamp punched-metal fixture hangs from the *boveda* ceiling over the island work top.

This landscape lantern lights the garden walk.

This three-shade fixture hangs over the kitchen counter.

A shaded six-light metal chandelier hangs in the center of the living room.

This punched-metal fixture hangs over the dining room table suspended from a *boveda* ceiling.

One of two coach lights adorning
either side of the entry.

This contemporary floor lamp lights up a corner of the dining room.

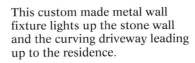

This custom made metal wall fixture lights up the stone wall and the curving driveway leading up to the residence.

This nine-light tubular metal fixture hangs over the dining table from a wood beam above.

Chapter 10
Ceilings & Floors ⤦ *Techos y Pisos*

The *boveda* ceiling is the most striking ceiling found in San Miguel. No matter the shape of the room, whether it is square, rectangular or round, the *boveda* ceiling is always a dome or barrel vault. Starting at the extreme edges, using light-weight bricks and no formwork, the master mason lays up a portion each day, working his way toward the center from all sides. This process is repeated until he puts in the last brick and viola, we have a paved looking ceiling. Some have a plain look while others can be more decorative with different colored brick or off-sets.

Not all *boveda* ceilings are without a design element.

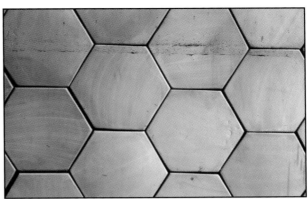

Hexagonal.

Hexagonal *Alargada*.

This domed brick *boveda* ceiling runs the entire length and width of the room.

119

Combinado 2 Picos

Combination *saltillo* and *talavera*.

This pattern is called *Quadrado*.

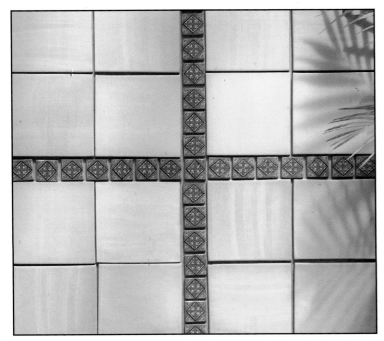

This is a variation on the previous pattern, *Quadrado* 20 x 20.

This *saltillo* tile with rocks in between in lieu of grout aids in drainage on this outdoor patio.

Combination hexagonal and square *saltillo* floor tiles.

121

Chapter 11
Stairways ∽ *Escaleras*

Some say the stairway is the vehicle to the stars. Here in San Miguel, stairways lead to the rooftop patios and expanded entertainment areas providing a magnificent view of the downtown skyline. The rooftop patio with a lush contingent of plants also provides a quiet place away from the street noises. *Talavera* tiles can be found embellishing most stairways giving the otherwise humdrum stair a colorful design change.

Right:
The outdoor fountain covered in colorful *talavera* tiles is framed in the quatrefoil window. The colorful walls of the stairway invade the senses.

Opposing page left:
A traditional stairway with balustrades, *saltillo* treads and *talavera* tile inlaid on the risers. Even though the balustrades are low, the flower pots *macetas* raise the visual height giving the descending person a higher comfort level.

Opposing page right:
Medio-panuelo tiles on risers.

The *talavera* tiles brighten up this stair with the combination *saltillo* and *talavera* treads and a magnificent mix of tile on the risers and top of the wall.

Simple but elegant interior stairway with graceful lines curving up to the second level.

This stairway landing sports a fireplace.

A powder room is snuggled below this stairway.

This three-story stairwell lights up brilliantly at night when these hanging paper globes are illuminated.

Saltillo treads with *talavera* tiles inlaid in concrete.

This *talavera* tile pattern on the risers is called *Concha tc*.

Approaching the main entrance to the street, the *talavera* tile pattern is named *violetas*, leads the eye to the yellow wall surrounding the door.

Medio-panuelo risers inlaid between *cantera* stone treads.

This stairway is lined with carved masks and hanging donkey tails.

The *fleur* designed *talavera* tile accents the risers in this stairway.

A traditional stairway with a modern touch and a wrought iron hand rail.

This grand staircase with its wrought iron railing is well lighted by two tall windows at the landing.

Chapter 12
Niches ☙ *Nichos*

Niches are found almost anywhere in the house where there is a blank wall. Traditionally, niches are used to display religious icons and figures of men of the cloth.

In addition, this recess in the wall provides a place for multiple uses not least of which are planters, recesses for furniture, and in the kitchen for cooking.

The bottom front light casts an interesting effect and shadow on this Asian sculpture.

A *nicho* top light shines down on this modern sculpture.

These *nichos* are lit at the bottom behind the objects of art displayed.

A classic plastered shell topped *nicho* holds a blue and white *talavera* urn.

In traditional Mexican kitchens, *nichos* were made under the counter top for storage as well as large *nichos* like this brick lined one with the *talavera* tile *murale*. Notice the *medio-panuelo* yellow and white tile counter front, and typical clay cookware.

This large *nicho* is decorated with a lighted plastered shell.

The back of this *nicho* has been painted to accent the *ratablo* de *santos* (altarpiece of saints).

The light in this *nicho* shines down on an antique religious figure.

Nichos are the perfect way to display many different kinds of special pieces.

The dark color of the back of the *nicho* makes this figure stand out.

A different kind of *nicho* holds a religious painting where two walls come together.

This *nicho* is edged and frames the figure inside.

The back blue wall of this *nicho* and the blue front line set off the folk art figure inside. The two painted clay suns complete the scene.

131

Chapter 13
Art * *Arte*

Art flourishes in the Mexican home whether it is folk art, art commemorating a holiday, religious or otherwise, a fiesta, or a point in time in Mexican history. Mexican artisans are creative and imaginative, using whatever materials are available. Much of the art found in homes depends on personal tastes and the excitement at the time one discovers a must-have one-of-a-kind treasure. There is a feeling among shoppers that if they see something that appeals to them, they should buy it at that time, for if they were to return later to purchase, that piece would be long gone.

This large wrought iron decorative candle holder can be used in the garden *jardin*.

This stuffed horse stands in a corner waiting for a friendly carrot.

Many whimsical creatures intricately painted adorn this clay figure from Oaxaca.

Unfired clay is often used in folk art pieces like this painted church.

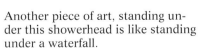

Another piece of art, standing under this showerhead is like standing under a waterfall.

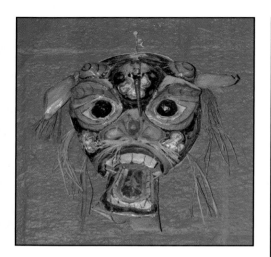

This fragile painted mask *mascara* is hung on the wall for safe keeping.

Religious art is a popular theme in decorating. Here old wood and tin crosses are displayed on a glass top table up against a stone wall.

Tin feathers surround the tin sun-faced mask with curled tin eye lashes and black marble eyes.

Masks are often painted glazed clay like this one.

A terracotta sun-faced mask with colorful bright matte colors.

This colorful painted mask *mascara* was carried in a parade.

Paper-mache chickens, some with eggs, are all different and fun folk art.

An unusual wall-mounted clay sculpture.

Very detailed clay and wood painted figures and scenes are highly collectible folk art.

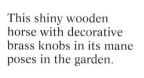

This shiny wooden horse with decorative brass knobs in its mane poses in the garden.

The artistic swirls and colors of onyx are featured in this sink.

This twisted candle holder used outdoors has a rusty finish which is popular for light fixtures, railings, and other decorative pieces.

This man-in-the-moon is a fabric wall hanging.

This paper-mache bird holds the owner's earrings.

137

Various sized nails were embedded into the wood backing to create this sculpture for a wall hanging.

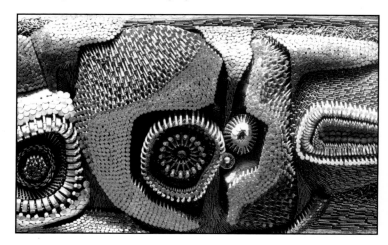

This is a close-up of a sculpture made with embedded nails into a wood background.

A whimsical collage creation surrounds this mirror.

These dance masks *mascara* are cleverly displayed on stands.

Dance masks *mascaras* are popular collectibles to display.

A popular religious art form to display is a *ratablo de santos* (altarpiece of saints).

Chapter 14
Talavera Ceramics & Tiles ⌁ Ceramicas y Ozulejas

The *talavera* displayed in the following photos were photographed either in homes here in San Miguel or stores *tiendas* in the nearby town of Delores Hidalgo. There are at least six major factory stores in Dolores Hidalgo, where one may find large selections of lead-free dinnerware, ceramic-framed mirrors, drawer knobs, tiles, sinks, candelabra, casseroles, bowls, platters, and ginger jars, to name just a few of the items available.

Showroom.

Showroom.

Showroom.

Platter.

A *talavera* fruit bowl.

141

Ginger jar approximately two feet tall.

Pattern zig zag.

Talavera urn.

Striped.

This *talavera* pottery with its green plant sits in a corner of the entry welcoming visitors.

This three-foot-tall ginger jar sits as a silent sentry just inside the entrance to the courtyard.

Another large jar on the rooftop patio enhances the views of downtown San Miguel.

This colorful *talavera* pottery with handles would lighten up any room.

Once fired pottery and dinnerware await design motifs and colorist.

Companion *talavera macetas* with plants sit at the entrance to the showroom.

It would be a shame to cover this patterned bowl with fruit.

Adding color prior to tin-glaze and second-time firing.

Tile index – some of the available tile patterns.

The *talavera* tiles brighten up this handrail and stair with the combination *talavera* and *saltillo* treads and a great combination of tiles on the risers.

A tile panel showing a variation on a theme.

Pyramids

Indio

Flor pattern.

145

Yet more *talavera* tile as a wainscot above the lavatory and behind the water closet.

The yellow and blue painted base cabinet front doors are a brilliant contrast to the *talavera* tile surrounding the doors as well as the top and the walls.

The magnificent mix of *talavera* tiles continues around to the bathtub.

This concrete bathtub with the *talavera* tile surrounding the Jacuzzi jets occupies one corner in this bathroom.

Creative use of the water closet matching the rest of the bathroom fixtures.

This *talavera* bowl matches the tile edging on the base cabinet along with the various containers sitting on the counter top.

147

Chapter 15
Color ❧ Color

San Miguel had been a place lacking in color-ful expression and, only recently, has blossomed forth in vibrant, bright colors. Along with its brilliant natural light and a cobalt blue sky matched no where else, San Miguel has emerged as if from a cocoon with its cornucopia of rainbow colors splashed on walls and rooftops. Mexicans have even painted their interior walls with the brightest colors as well. The use of bright colors was introduced by the famous Mexican *arquitecto*, Luis Barragan, and today has been carried forth by young aspiring Mexican architects. Color definitely reflects the Mexican spirit found here. Color is everywhere.
The paint colors used in this chapter, together with the various creative works, are available from paint stores. You only need to show a sample of the color you want and they will come very close to matching it.

Color swatches above are, from left to right, Pantone® numbers 812U and 172U.

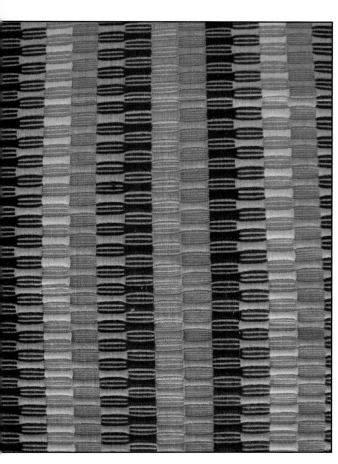

Color swatches above are, from the top, Pantone® numbers 172U, 807U, and 7409U.

Color swatches at right are, from left to right, Pantone® numbers Hexachrome BlackU, 137U, and 7414U.

149

Color swatches at right are, from the top, Pantone® numbers 123U, 172U, and 191U.

Color swatches below are, from left to right, Pantone® numbers 116U, Orange 021U, and 718U.

Color swatches at the right are, from the top, Pantone® numbers 661U and Orange 021U.

150

Color swatches at right are, from the top, Pantone® numbers Red 032U, 3955U, and Blue 072U.

Color swatches above are, from left to right, Pantone® numbers 485U, 813U, 107U, 351U, 7455U.

Color swatches at the right are, from the top, Pantone® numbers 807U, 123U, and Orange 021U.

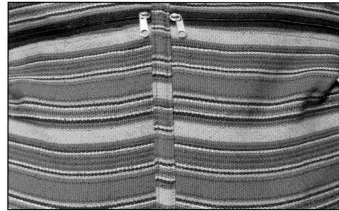

Glossary ∽ Glosario

Agua. Water
A la derecha. To the right
Alberca. Pool
Amigo. Friend
Arboles. Trees
Arcada. Arcade
Armario. Cabinet
Arquitecto. Architect
Artes. Arts
Azul. Blue
Azulejo. Tile

Balaustrada. Balustrade
Banco. Bench
Bandidos. Bandits
Baño. Bathroom
Boveda. Vault
Brasero. Brazier

Canalon. Gutter
Cantera. Volcanic stone
Cantina. Bar
Cartas. Letters
Casa. House
Cascada. Waterfall
Casita. Small house
Catrina. Female skeleton
Chimenea. Fireplace
Clavo. Nail
Cobalto. Colbalt
Cochera. Garage
Cocina. Kitchen
Columna. Column
Comal. Earthen pot
Comedor. Dining room
Comoda. Chest of drawers
Cornisa. Cornice

Corredor. Corridor
Cristo. Christ
Cupula. Cupola or dome

Entrada. Entryway
Equipale. Pigskin furniture
Escalera. Stairway

Fabrica. Fabricate
Fachada. Facade
Flores. Flowers
Fuenta. Fountain

Hierro. Iron
Hombre. Man

Iglesia. Church
Iluminacion. Lighting

Jardin. Garden
Jarrones. Large jars

Laja. Flat rock
Llamador. Door

Maceta. Flowerpot
Maestro. Master craftsman
Mariachi. Mariachi street band
Mascara. Mask
Mensula. Bracket
Moldura. Molding

Nicho. Niche

Ojo. Eye

Petates. Reed mats
Petatillo. A thin brick

Pilar. Pillar
Portal. Foyer
Portico. Covered porch at entry
Porton. Large door
Postigo. Small door usually inside another door
Puerta. Door

Recamara. Bedroom
Reja. Iron grating or railing
Retablo. Religious painting

Sala. Living room
Santo. Saint
Silla. Chair
Sillar. A masonry unit a little larger than a 8"x 8"x 16" concrete block
Sillon. Couch

Tablero. Panel of tiles
Talavera. Hand-painted, twice-fired, tin-glazed earthenware
Troje. Wooden house

Vestibulo. Hall or public lobby
Viga. Beam or girder

Zaguan. Passage from street to inner courtyard
Zocalo. Baseboard

Resources ❦ Recursos

LIFESTYLE

FOOD & TABLETOP

Bonanza
Mesones 43
152 1260
A complete in-town supermarket with
hard to find imported ítems.

De Talavera
Puebla No. 60 esq.
Tamaulipas
Delores Hidalgo, Gto.
(418) 182 0749
An extensive line of *talavera* dinner-
ware.

La Buena Vida
H Macias 72
152 2211
Bakery & Cafe
Natural whole grain breads, French
baguettes and unique pastries.

La Europea
Canal 13
152 2003
An extensive selection of wines and
spirits.

Maxi Vinos
Zacateros 84
152 2219
A good selection of wines and spirits.

Petitfour
Mesones 99
154 4010
Pastry shop, bar and café. Homemade
chocolates, cakes, pies and French
pastries.

FURNITURE

Arden Casa de Muebles
Libr. Celaya a Delores 26
154 8010
Furniture and home decor accessories.

Camila
Sollano 30
152 2697
Antique furniture, etched glass, cus-
tom-made linens & tablecloths.

Casa Canal
Canal 3
152 0479
Hand-carved Furniture.

Casa del Inquisidor
Aldama 1
154 6868
Household accessories and an extensive hardware selection.

Casa Marie Luisa
Ancha Sn Antonio 26
152 2983
Furniture and home decor accessories.

Coba Art Décor
Juarez 7
154 7516
Interior design, accessories and fine furniture from India.

Colección Cuatro Vientos
Sollano 31
154 9132
Furniture and home decor accessories.

C. Dewayne Youts
Fabrica la Aurora
152 5481
Manufacturing of wood and iron furniture, 17th century reproductions, custom kitchens and accessories.

El Progresso
Road to Delores Hidalgo
(418) 120 3048
Hand-crafted furniture.

Evos
H Macias 55
152 0813
Classic San Miguel style home furnishings, Spanish colonial furniture, imported sofas, upholstered furniture, fabrics, and oriental rugs.

Finca
Fabrica la Aurora
154 8323
Furniture, accessories and interiors.

Hacienda la Diligencia
H. Macias 118
152 1626
Custom furniture made to your design and specifications.

Manuel Padron
Santa Clara
Progresso2004@prodigy.net.mx
Hand-crafted furniture.

Marcia Bland Brown
Hacienda Calderón
044 415 153 3176
Furniture design & manufacturing, antiques, interior & architectural design and restoration.

Namuh Collection
Camino Alcocer Km 2.2
154 8080
Indoor/outdoor furniture and accessories from Asia.

SHOPS

Antigua Casa Canela
Umaran 20
152 1880
Antiques, Colonial art and home décor accessories.

Artes de México
Calzada de la Aurora 47
152 0764
Mexican arts and crafts, tin ornaments, Colonial furniture and folk art.

ArtesMéxico
Zacateros 81A
154 8531
Quality hand-wrought copper.

Azulejos Talavera Cortes S.A. de C.V.
Aldama No. 18
Delores Hidalgo, C.I.N., GTO., México
(418) 182 1168
Finest glazed *talavera* tiles for floor finishing as well as an infinite range of accessories.

Buenas Noches
Fabrica la Aurora
154 9624
Fine bed and bath furnishings.

Cantadora
Fabrica la Aurora
154 8302
Cantera, fireplaces, columns, door frames and decorative accessories.

Carrillo Vertix Hermanos
Puebla No. 54
Delores Hidalgo, C.I.N., GTO., México
(418) 182 0122
Talavera tiles, traditional and Barcelona, murals and accessories.

Casa Coloniales
Canal 36
152 0286
Furniture, upholstery, fabrics, trim, pillows, spreads, curtains, rugs, chandeliers, sconces, stone ornaments and gifts.

Casa Roberto
Libr a Queretaro 35
152 8620
Lighting, ceiling fans, water filters, purifier, radiant heaters and fireplace accessories.

Galería Tesoro
Recreo 8B
154 5595
Folk art and home decor accessories.

Icpalli
Correo 43
152 1236
Fabric for interior design, window treatment, furniture and home accessories.

Icons
Pila Seca 3
152 5762
Traditional Byzantine Images.

Ilumina San Miguel
Calzada de la Luz 51
154 7643
Commercial & residential lighting,
chandeliers, lamps
and sconces.

Lan Art
Ancha de San Antonio
152 1566
Rugs, bedspreads, pillows and household accessories.

La Victoriana
H Macias 72
152 6903
Botanical beauty products, herbal and
homeopathic remedies, flower essence
and aromatherapy.

La Zandunga
H Macias 129
152 4608
Fine Mexican rugs.

Mitu Atelier
Sollano 32
044 415 117 9431
Home accessories, custom furniture
and antiques.

Productos Herco, S.A.
Relox #12
152 1434
A large selection of faucets, sinks, bath
tubs in various materials including copper and marble, decorative hardware
and kitchen accessories.

Sisal
Fabrica la Aurora
154 8944
Home decor and interior design.

Sollano 16
Sollano 16
154 8872
Lifestyle & home décor and accessories.

Talavera Vázquez
Puebla No. 56
Delores Hidalgo, C.I.N., GTO., México
(418) 182 2914
Talavera tiles, flowerpots, murals and
earthenware.

Zocalo
H Macias 110
152 0663
Fine Mexican folk art and furniture and
hand-blown glassware.

BOOKSELLERS
Casa de Papel
Mesones 57
154 5187
Greeting cards, journals, photo al-
bums, candles, guide books, road maps,
Mexican cook books, prints, posters
and CDs.

El Colibi
Sollano30
152 0751
Spanish language books, art books and
artist's materials.

El Pato
M Ledesma 19
152 1543
Art supplies, design & accessories.

Lagundi
Umaran 17
152 0830
Art supplies, frames and framing, posters, original prints, books and magazines.

Libros el Tecolote
Jesús 11
152 7395
English language books, Mexican history, literature, art & design books.

SERVICES
Fortuna
Pila Seca 3
152 7782
Specialists in conservation & preservation of fine art, photographs, textiles and memorabilia.

INFORMATION
Atencion
Insurgentes 25
152 3770

Promoción Mexican culture (PMC)
Hidalgo 18
152 0121
Tourist Information

WEARABLE ART

Barbara Porter
Zacateros 47
152 7463
Fashion designs for men & women.

Black & White
Loreto 20
154 4493
Traveling clothes, *alpaca* sweaters and accessories.

Caracol Collection
Cuadrante 30
152 1617
Fine and applied art, furniture, arte copper and ceramics.

Christofas
Cuadrante 2
154 9392
Unique designer jewelry, sculpture, décor art, mobiles and gemstones.

Creación Marcela Andre
Sn Francisco 7
154 9868
Original art, jewelry and decorations.

Diva
H Macias 72
152 4980
Jewelry, accessories and creative quality clothes in European linens.

Girasol
Sn Francisco 72
152 2734
Mexican casuals

Goldie Designs
Zacateros 19
154 7521
Classic clothing, elegant jewelry and custom accessories

Nuevo México
Aparicio 1
152 4510
Navajo style crafts

7th Heaven
Sollano 13
154 4677
Unique jewelry, art, gifts and clothes

GALLERIES

Atenea Gallery
Jesús 2
152 0785
Paintings, sculpture, graphics, jewelry and art objects.

Casa Diana Art Gallery
Recreo 48
152 0885
An exclusive art gallery featuring paintings and sculpture.

Galería Aspen
Mesones 74
154 4441
Investment art.

Galería Izamal
Mesones 80
154 5409
Paintings and jewelry design by local artists in this cooperative gallery.

Galería Mariposa
Recreo 36
152 4488
Specializing in one of a kind pieces by the great masters of Mexican folk Art.

Galería Pérgola
Instituto Allende
154 5595
Mexican fine art

Galería San Miguel
Plaza Principle 14
152 0454
Contemporary works of art.

Generator Gallery
Fabrica la Aurora
154 9588

Whitfield gallery
Sn Francisco 18
150 0094
Fine art.

Bibliography ∽ Bibliografía

Barragan, The Complete Works. New York: Princeton Architectural Press, 1996.

de Haro, Fernando and Omar Fuentes. *Arquitectos Mexicanos, Una Visipn Contemporanea.* México D.F.: Arquitectos Mexicanos Editores S.A. de C.V., 2004.

_____. *Mexican Interiors*: *Style & Personality*. México D.F.: Arquitectos Mexicanos Editores S.A. de C.V., 2003.

Levick, Melba and Gina Hyams. *Mexicasa, The Enchanting Inns and Haciendas of Mexico*. San Francisco: Chronicle Books, 2001.

Levick, Melba, Tony Cohan and Masako Takahashi. *Mexicolor: The Spirit of Mexican Design*. San Francisco: Chronicle Books, 1998.

Luscombe-Whyte, Mark and Dominic Bradbury. *Mexico Architecture, Interiors & Design*. New York: Harper Collins Publishers, 2004.

Stoeltie, Barbara and Rene Stoeltie. *Living in Mexico: Vivre au Mexique:* Cologne: Taschen, 2004.

Streeter-Porter, Tim. *Casa Mexicana: The Architecture, Design and Style of Mexico*. New York: Stewart, Tabori & Chang, 1994.

Villela, Khristaan, Ellen Bradbury and Logan Wagner. *Contemporary Mexican Design and Architecture*. Layton, Utah: GibbsSmith, Publisher, 2002.

Yampolsky, Mariana and Chloe Sayer. *The Traditional Architecture of Mexico*. New York: Thames and Hudson, 1993.

Ypma, Herbert. *Mexican Contemporary*. New York: Stewart, Tabori & Chang, 1997.